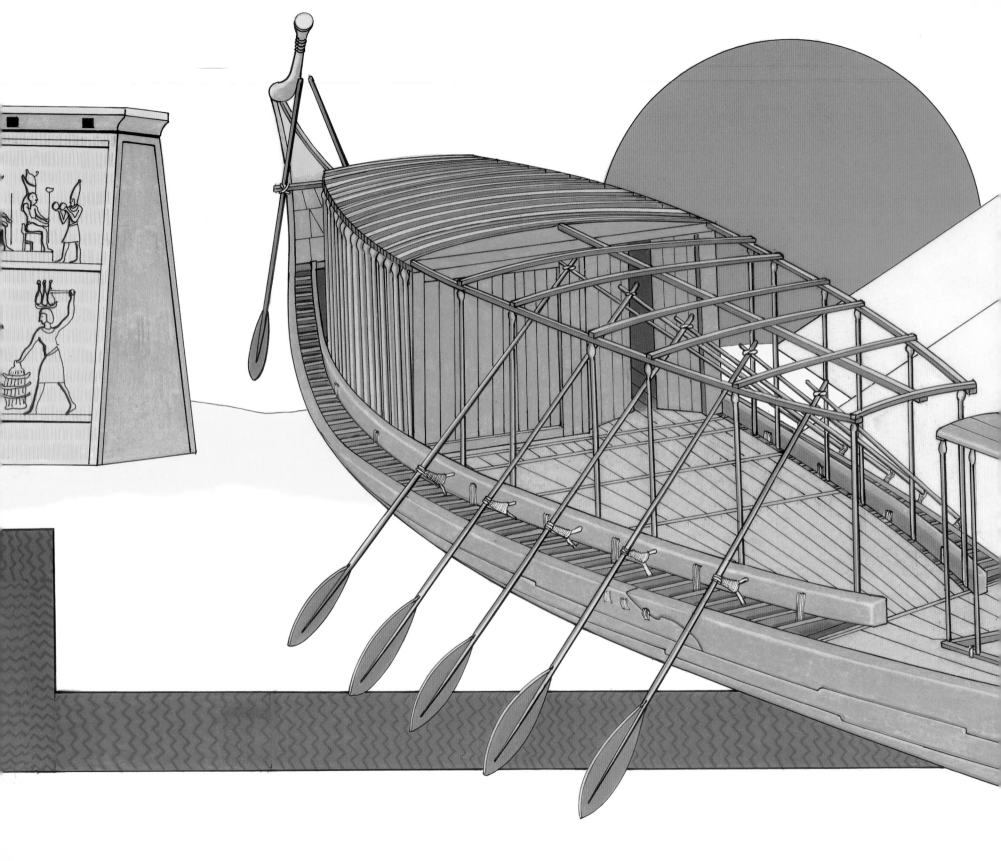

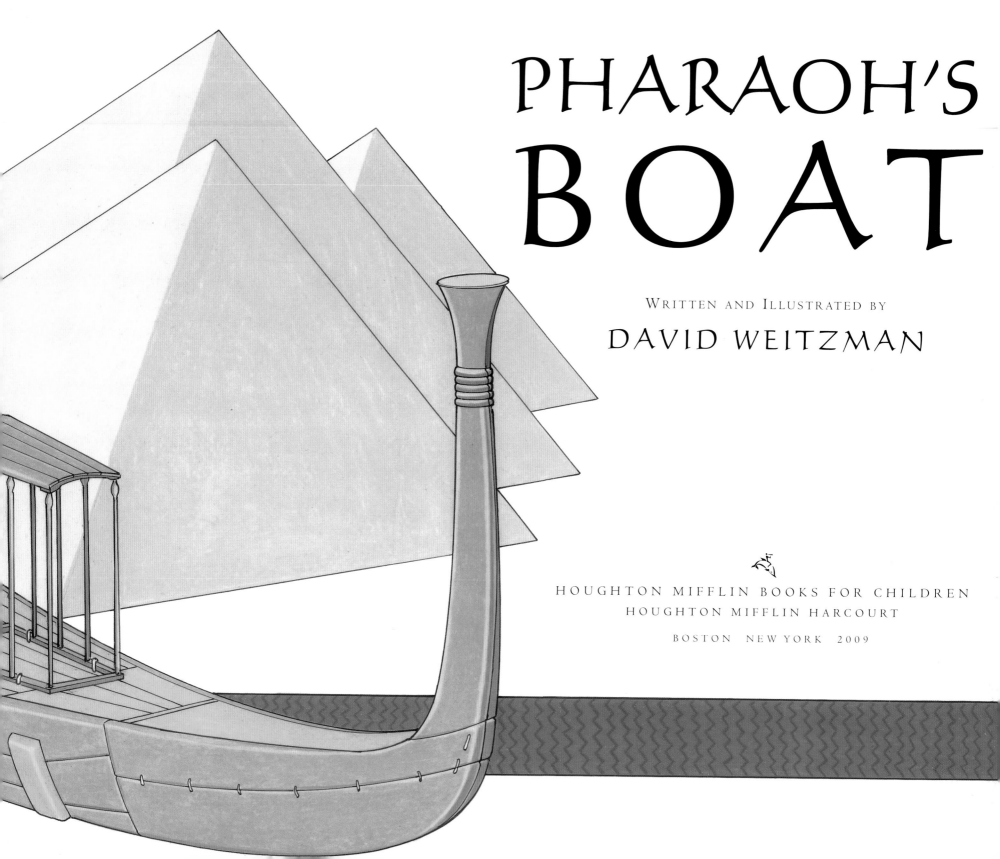

PHARAOH'S BOAT

WRITTEN AND ILLUSTRATED BY

DAVID WEITZMAN

HOUGHTON MIFFLIN BOOKS FOR CHILDREN
HOUGHTON MIFFLIN HARCOURT

BOSTON   NEW YORK   2009

For Hag Ahmed Youssef Moustafa

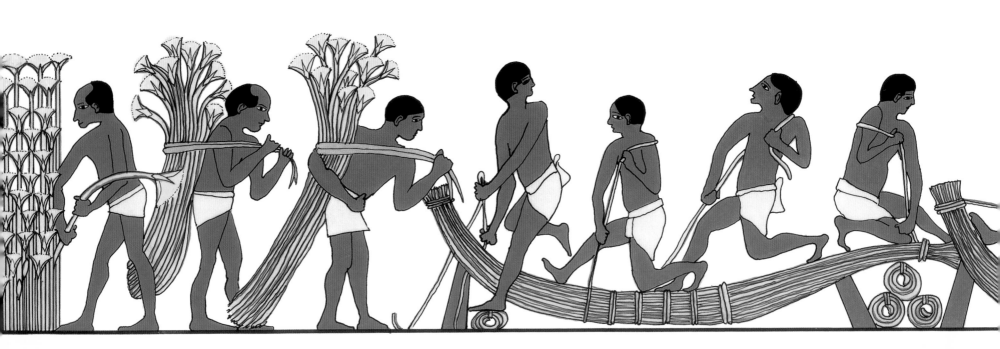

Prologue

In 1954, workmen began clearing away tons of windblown sand and rubble that had piled up against the south face of the Great Pyramid at Giza. As they dug, there suddenly appeared an old stone boundary wall. Strange. They weren't expecting to find a wall here. It was closer to the pyramid's base than the boundary walls on the northern, eastern, and western sides.

Kamel el Mallakh, the Egyptologist supervising the work, was puzzled. The ancient Egyptian builders were always so precise about placing structures, he was certain this was not a mistake. Had the wall been deliberately built there to hide something?

The pharaoh, Cheops, is dead, the people lament.
Now we are like a ship adrift without oars.
There will be only chaos, and the sun
will not appear in the sky tomorrow.

Pharaoh, the Egyptians believed, was divine: all knowing, all powerful, in word and deed perfect in every way. The moment Cheops became pharaoh he also became a deity, a son of Re, the sun god. "Thou art like Re in all thou doest," his subjects would say upon entering the royal presence, foreheads to the ground. "Everything happens according to the wish of thy heart."

And everything did. In preparation for his own death, Cheops, like his father before him, ordered an enormous pyramid built to shelter everything he would need in the afterlife. But his pyramid would be even grander. Over the next twenty years, a hundred thousand workers cut, finished, and transported some 2,300,000 stone blocks weighing as much as fifteen tons, and raised them up to create a pyramid almost five hundred feet high.

On the day Cheops died, 4,600 years ago, it was ready for him. But there was one more task to be done.

Nun, god of the rivers and oceans, held aloft the boat of the rising sun. Re—sometimes in his human form, sometimes as a scarab beetle, and sometimes with the head of a hawk—ferried it through the heavens.

YOU COME TO LIFE A SECOND TIME.

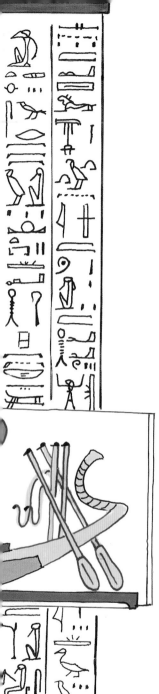

Djedefre, Cheops's son, succeeded his father as pharaoh, and his first concerns were the rituals that would assure his father's safe passage into the afterlife. He ordered the construction of two magnificent ships: one to guide Cheops safely through the dark, perilous underworld of night, and the other to carry him up across the sky to embark on his eternal journey with the sun.

Travel by boat was so intrinsic to the Egyptian way of life that it shaped the people's beliefs about this world— and the next. When the Egyptians looked up into the sky, they saw a vast sea, a heavenly river. During the day, the sun sailed across this sea on a ship guided by Re. At night they imagined millions of little boats floating across the black waters with bright lanterns—the moon and stars—at their bows.

Re's sun boat was crewed by pharaohs who upon their death were judged by the gods to be worthy of eternal life. Inscribed on the inside of their coffins were texts from the Book of the Dead, which protected them on their perilous journey to the afterworld and explained their service to Re. The pharaoh might help row the sun westward, chanting, "I take my oar; I row Re," or as captain, navigate the solar boat by the stars, saying, "I command the god's bark for him; steer his bark; I will fare upstream at the bow; I will guide the voyages."

Like many cultures, the ancient Egyptians believed the dead had to journey across a body of water, a "winding waterway," to arrive at the afterlife. And so, to reach the sun god there on the other side, Cheops, like other pharaohs before him, would need boats of his own.

Djedefre could be sure that his father's boats would be built with time-proven craftsmanship. The Egyptians were expert builders of all kinds of boats, from little skiffs made of bundled papyrus reeds to huge wooden ships that were powered by woven cotton sails and leaf-shaped oars.

Instead of a rudder, two large steering oars at the stern controlled the direction of travel. The boats fairly skimmed over the surface of the water, with the rowers at their oars, or the

crew clambering aloft to work the lines and the billowing papyrus sails, and the captain at the helm.

Few trees big enough for ships' timbers grow in Egypt. But the Nile River served as a great highway, connecting cities along its banks with other peoples and goods on the shores of the Mediterranean Sea. Trading fleets sailed far and wide to bring back cedar, sycamore, and acacia trunks for shipbuilding, and the very finest were selected for Pharaoh's boat.

When the timbers arrived, the master shipbuilder needed no plans to begin his wooden masterpiece. In his powerful, gnarled hands was the knowledge of centuries of boat building tradition. He simply took up his "pencil," a twig dipped in charcoal, and drew the outline of the first plank on a cedar log. Cedar was perfect for building ships because it was easy to work and resistant to decay and ship worms, which eat and live in wood.

The ancient shipwrights fashioned huge, sleek ships from the trunks and branches with a few simple bronze tools. Following the master builder's lines, craftsmen roughed out the ship's timbers with axes. Then, with an adz, they carefully chopped away at the uneven surface until they had the exact shape they wanted. When a plank needed to be sawn down its length, the worker lashed it to a post

and jammed a weighted stick between the windings to make them tight. Builders could drill holes with a simple back-and-forth motion of the bow drill.

Workmen cut thousands of slots into the planks with knife-sharp bronze chisels that they drove into the wood with heavy clubs. Because bronze is a soft metal and the chisels quickly dulled, the shipwrights always had a sharpening stone and horn filled with oil at hand. Finally, woodworkers scrubbed flat pieces of sandstone back and forth along the grain of the timber to smooth out the tool marks left by the axes and adzes until the surface was polished.

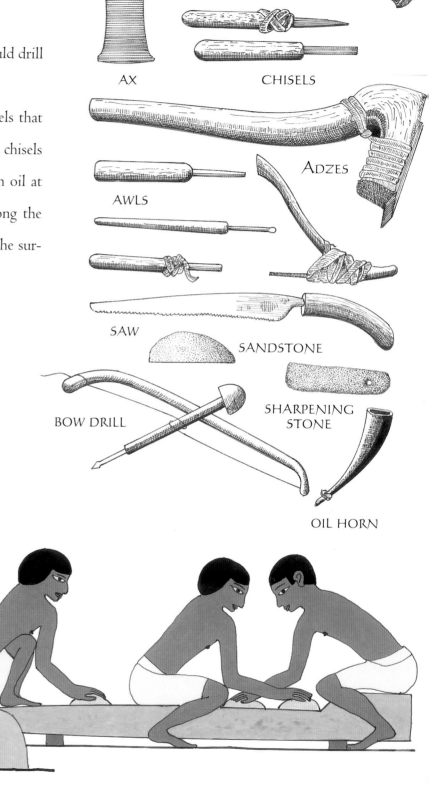

AX

CHISELS

ADZES

AWLS

SAW

SANDSTONE

BOW DRILL

SHARPENING STONE

OIL HORN

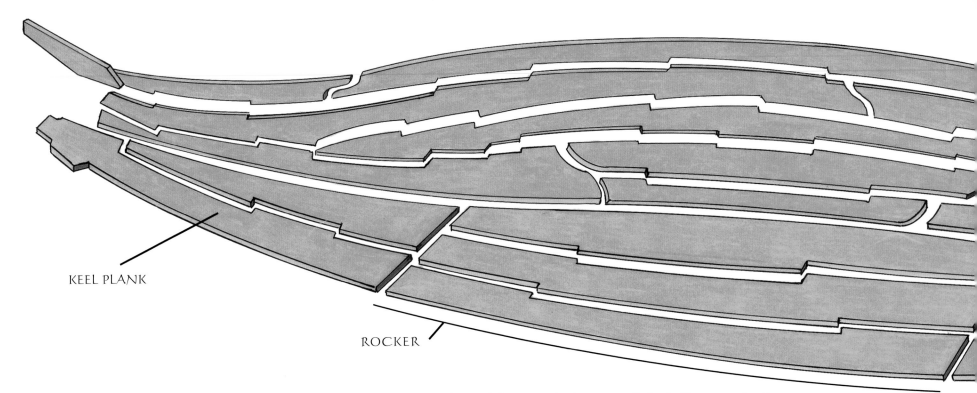

KEEL PLANK

ROCKER

The keel planks—the eight lengths of wood forming the bottom of the hull—were the first to be cut, laid out on the ground, and fastened together. Because the channel of the Nile was constantly changing, and much of it not very deep, Pharaoh's boat, like all the Nile river craft, would have a shallow draft so that very little of the hull sat below the water line.

Next, the workmen formed the rocker, the fore-to-aft curve of the hull. Stout ropes were fastened to the ends of the planks and drawn over a forked post. The workmen pushed sticks between the strands of rope and twisted them around and around. As the ropes tightened, they grew shorter and pulled up the ends of the planks. When the shipwrights had the curve they wanted, the rope was kept taut and pieces of wood were wedged under the keel planks until the planks had set in their new curve.

The rocker helped determine the boat's shape. Using this curve as their template, the boat builders could fashion the many pieces that would form the hull. The planks were joined end to end with S-shaped scarf joints. Toggles—tabs that fit into slots cut into adjoining pieces—locked all the planks together.

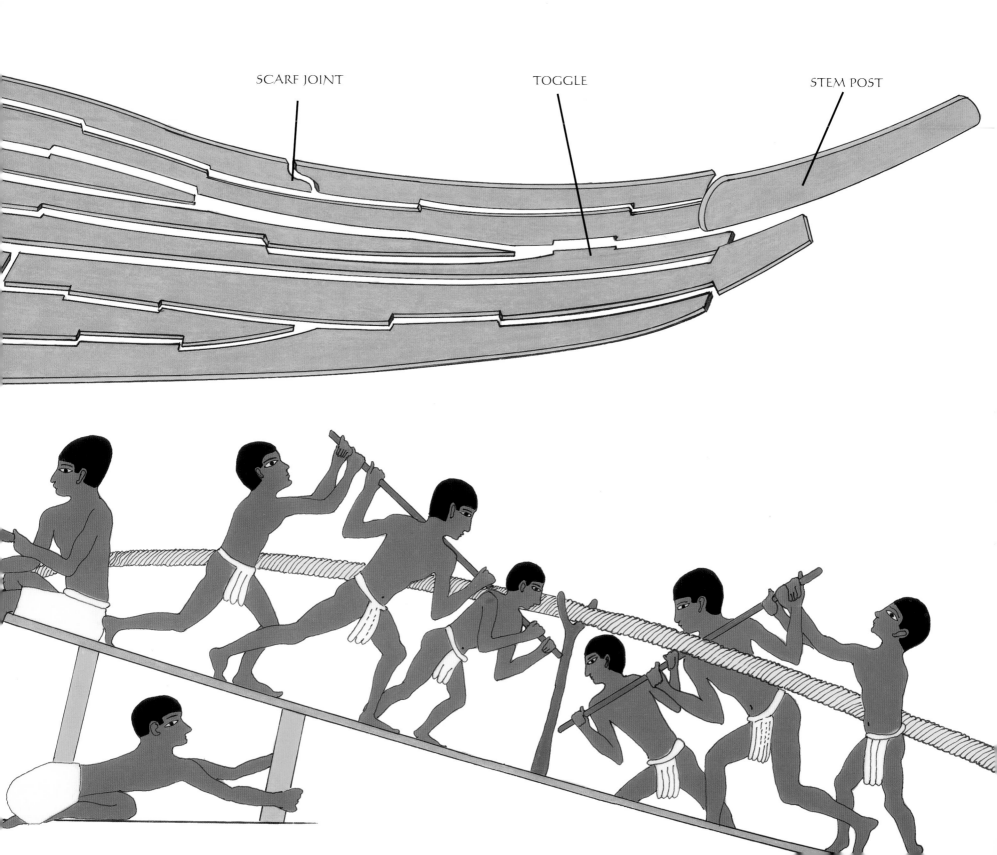

SCARF JOINT   TOGGLE   STEM POST

Teams of workers then cut and laid each of the long, heavy planks edge on edge, bent them to fit the curve of the hull, and temporarily lashed them together.

Once all the planks were assembled, battens—half-round lengths of wood—covered all the seams to keep water out. Then the entire ship was sewn together with rope woven from grasses and laced through more than four thousand V-shaped slots cut into the planks. While some workers tugged mightily on the rope, others beat on the lashing to help make it tighter.

The rope lashing did more than just hold the hull together. When sewn ships like this were launched, the wood soaked up water like a sponge and expanded. At the same time, the rope shrank as it got wet, pulling the planks together and closing any little spaces between them to make the ship watertight.

Sewn ships were strong, but they could also be easily disassembled, transported across the desert, and then reassembled on the shore of the Red Sea. From here they could sail south, toward the horn of Africa.

Archaeologists have found drawings, inscriptions, and bas-reliefs—pictures carved in stone—describing how the ancient boat builders sewed boats together. Hieroglyphs were written and read up, down, right to left, and, like these, left to right.

SAW THE PLANKS FROM CEDAR WOOD, ASSEMBLE THE PIECES, AND BIND WITH ROPE MADE OF REEDS. SHAPE AND BIND THE BOAT LIKE A PAPYRUS BOAT AND SEE HOW BEAUTIFUL IT IS.

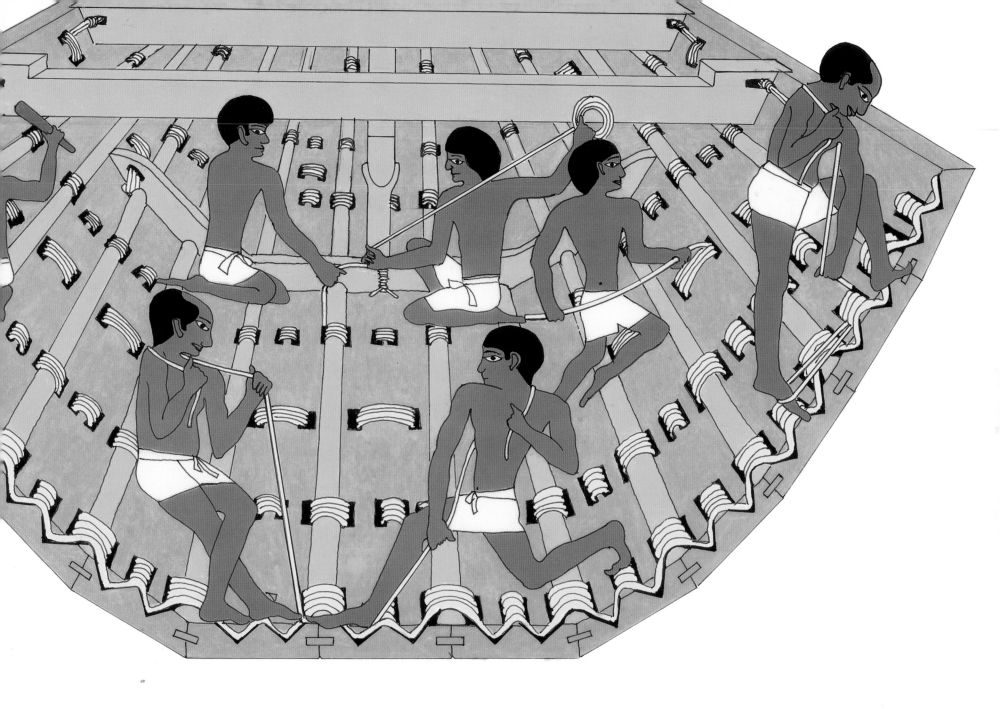

SHAPE THE PIECES AND BIND THEM TOGETHER WITH AX AND ADZ.

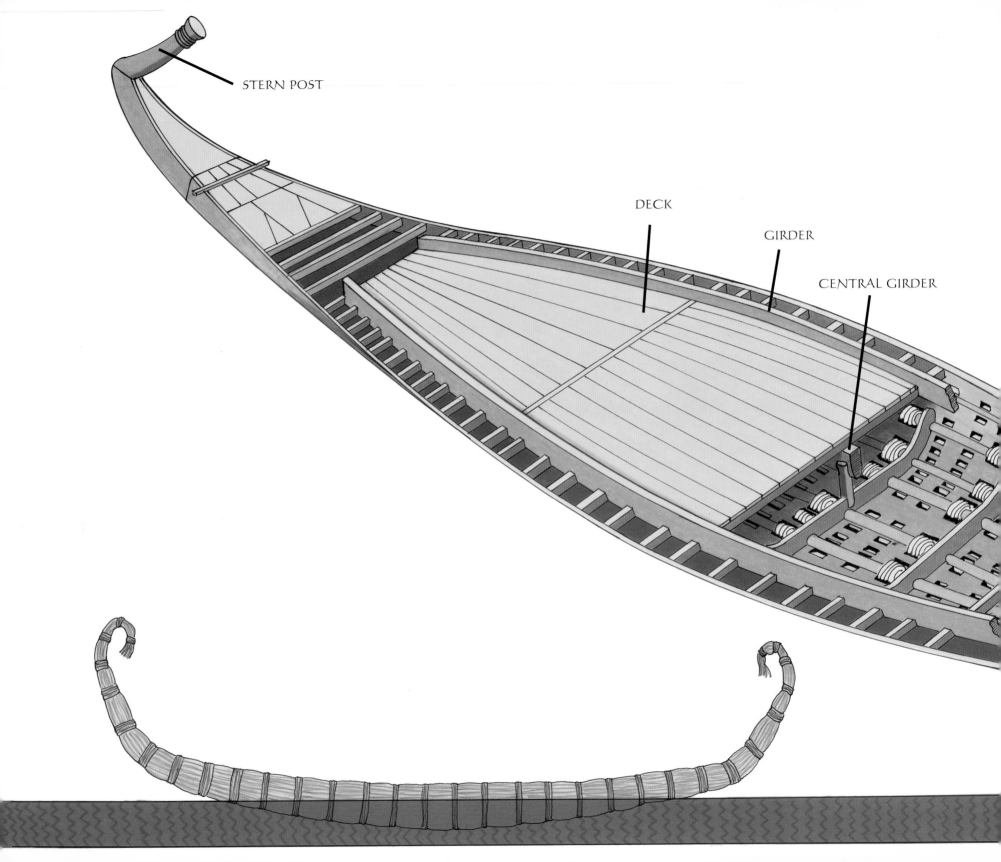

STERN POST

DECK

GIRDER

CENTRAL GIRDER

After the hull was sewn together, the shipwrights built an internal framework of timbers. A central girder—the ship's "spine"—ran the length of the ship just under the deck, with notches in it to hold each of the fifty deck beams that tied the uppermost planks together. The last two frame members, attached with rope, were the long, curved girders running along both sides of the deck. The hull was now complete, all without a single nail.

The gracefully curved posts at the bow and stern of Pharaoh's boat recreate in wood the traditional shape of Nile boats made of bundled papyrus reeds.

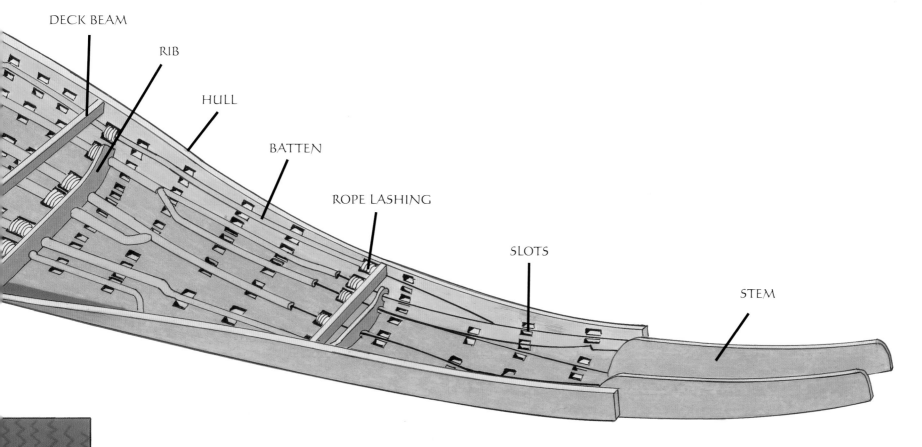

DECK BEAM

RIB

HULL

BATTEN

ROPE LASHING

SLOTS

STEM

As Cheops's boats neared completion under the watchful eye of Vizier Hemiunu, Overseer of All the King's Works, the shipwrights' craft was visible in every curve and joint of the golden cedar hull. Every plank formed two curves—the roundness of the hull and the long curve fore to aft—and every surface and edge was angled just so. The result was a smooth, graceful, river-worthy boat meant to last through the ages.

While Cheops's funerary ships were being finished, workers carved two pits—each a hundred feet long, eight feet wide, and eleven feet deep—out of the solid limestone bedrock at the base of his pyramid.

As soon as the boats were completed, they were taken apart and placed in the pits. To help Pharaoh reassemble them in the afterlife, the pieces were laid in thirteen orderly layers aligned with the path of the sun's travel—bow to the west, stern to the east. Starboard beams and planks were placed to the right, port beams and planks on the left. The workers even included lengths of rope to bind all the pieces together, woven matting, and a few tools.

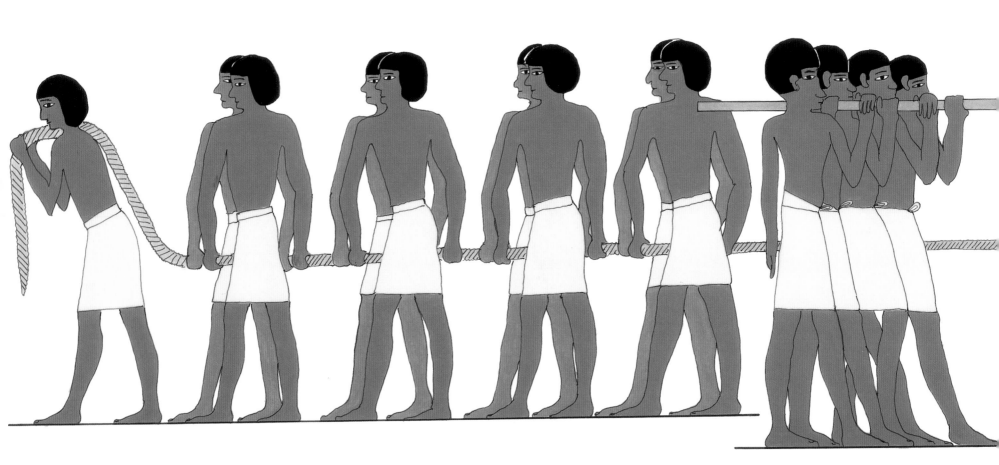

Meanwhile, throughout the construction period, the priests responsible for the dead had been meticulously following the rituals that prepared Cheops's body for life after death. Hundreds of artisans had been working to finish the wooden case that would hold his mummy, the paintings and bas-reliefs in his tomb, furniture, chariots, weapons, miniature granaries, and workshops—everything he would need in the afterlife. His body purified and preserved, Cheops would soon be making his last journey in this world, from his palace at Thebes down the Nile to his pyramid tomb at Giza, where his boats would be waiting for him.

As the boat pits were being prepared at the foot of Cheops's pyramid, stonemasons labored to cut the huge blocks that would cover them. Copper and bronze chisels were too soft to cut through the rock, so the quarrymen used tools of dolerite, an extremely hard stone.

Each block was pried away from the rock face and then all the sides made flat. The quarrymen then "signed" the stones by chiseling their personal marks, as well as Djedefre's, into each block. Then the stones were moved to the boat pits.

Workers easily moved the heavy stones by placing logs—which acted as little wheels—in front of and under the stones as they were moved across the sand.

One by one, the limestone blocks were set in a row over Cheops's ships, and every crack sealed with mortar. Although the air temperature in the desert is often hotter than one hundred degrees Fahrenheit, the air in the limestone pit stayed twenty or thirty degrees cooler. And because the limestone bedrock wicks moisture from groundwater below, the decay-resistant royal cedar can survive for thousands of years in this damp environment.

Finally, to protect the boats from robbers, the blocks were covered by a boundary wall encircling the pyramid. Here, if all went well, Cheops's ships would remain, available to him through all eternity.

When moving the stones on clay, workers heaved the stones up onto sleds and made the ground underneath slippery by pouring water just in front of the skids. In this way, immense stones could be moved great distances.

That might have been the end of the story were it not for one of those accidents to which archaeologists owe so much. In 1954, workmen were removing heaps of sand blown against the south face of the pyramid and piles of rubble left from earlier archaeological digs. They dug not with bulldozers but slowly and carefully with shovels, trowels, and their hands, alert for any artifacts that might still be buried. That's when they discovered the old boundary wall where they least expected to find it. The other three boundary walls were precisely 23.6 meters from the base of the pyramid; this southern wall was 5 meters closer.

Kamel el Mallakh, the Egyptologist supervising the work, found this intriguing. The ancient Egyptian builders were always so precise about their measurements; why, then, this variation? Continuing to dig down to what should have been bedrock, workmen instead found two rows of massive limestone blocks. Because the blocks were arranged in long rows, Malakh was certain they covered boat pits.

Chipping away at the mortar between two of the blocks, Mallakh cautiously dug a small hole down, down, down, until suddenly he broke through to the darkness below. "I smelled incense," Mallakh later recalled. "I smelled time, I smelled centuries, I smelled history. And then I was sure the boat was there." What he smelled was cedar as fragrant as if it had been placed there the year before. Reflecting the sun's light down into the pit with his shaving mirror—"the beam of Re," he says—he caught the first glimpse of a leaf-shaped oar.

Ahmed Youssef Moustafa, chief of the Restoration Department of the Egyptian Antiquities Service, was chosen to direct the recovery, preservation, and reconstruction of the huge ancient ship—an almost impossible task that no one had ever undertaken before.

When he was young, most of the archaeologists working in Egypt were foreigners, and Ahmed had dreamed of being one of the first Egyptians to explore and recover Egypt's glorious past. While still a teenager, Ahmed earned a first-class degree at Cairo's Institute of Applied Arts. Working on his own, he also taught himself the exacting work of restoration. But when he presented himself at the Egyptian Antiquities Service, hoping to be offered work as a restorer, he was handed a broom! He often asked to be allowed to try his hand at restoration. The answer was always no. Instead, he was given little plaster statuettes of Queen Nefertiti to paint to be sold later in the gift shop. Still, he persisted. "I made trouble at the department," he recalled years later with a smile and a twinkle in his eye.

[I have come] to the conclusion that the only way to assure success was to pretend to be

No longer able to tolerate the young man's unending questions and insistence on helping, the museum's curator gave him a box containing a clod of dirt-caked fragments of wood, ivory, and glazed pottery. The curator sent him away and instructed him not to return until he made something of the pieces, confident—Ahmed believed—they had seen the last of him.

At home he carefully cleaned the chips and arranged them in different patterns. He made drawings of his reconstructions, tried new arrangements, made more drawings. A month later he returned to the museum and placed in the curator's hands an exquisite little ebony box inlaid with tiny pieces of blue pottery and ivory. The Akhenaten Box, as it became known, is on display at the Cairo Museum, considered one of Egypt's treasures.

Over the next twenty years Ahmed became an expert restoration specialist, recording and restoring important tombs. And now he was about to take on one of the most important projects in the history of Egyptian archaeology.

the ancient maker, to retrace his steps, and do again what he did long ago in moulding his masterpiece.

—Hag Ahmed Youssef Moustafa

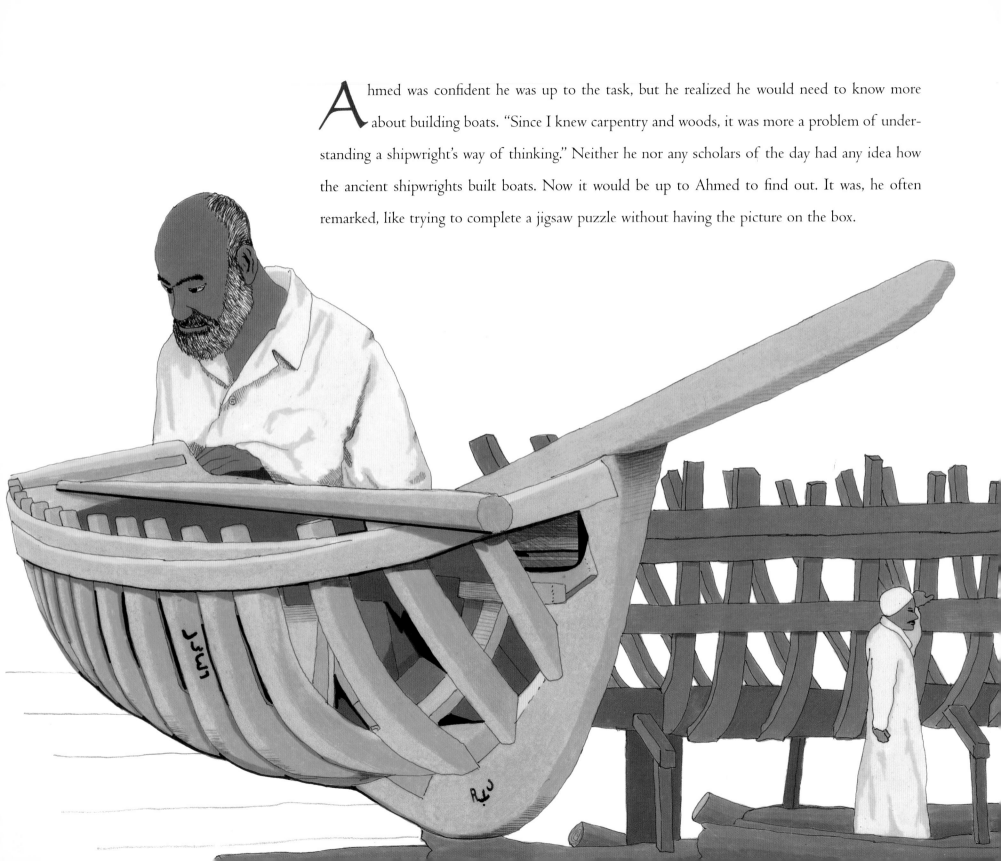

Ahmed was confident he was up to the task, but he realized he would need to know more about building boats. "Since I knew carpentry and woods, it was more a problem of understanding a shipwright's way of thinking." Neither he nor any scholars of the day had any idea how the ancient shipwrights built boats. Now it would be up to Ahmed to find out. It was, he often remarked, like trying to complete a jigsaw puzzle without having the picture on the box.

So Ahmed apprenticed himself to some local boat builders. He visited their boatyard, watched, asked questions, made sketches, and took a turn doing some of the work. Then he hired one of the men to look over his shoulder while he built scale models of their market boats. Later, the scale model he built of the pharaoh's boat would help him solve difficult problems of reconstruction.

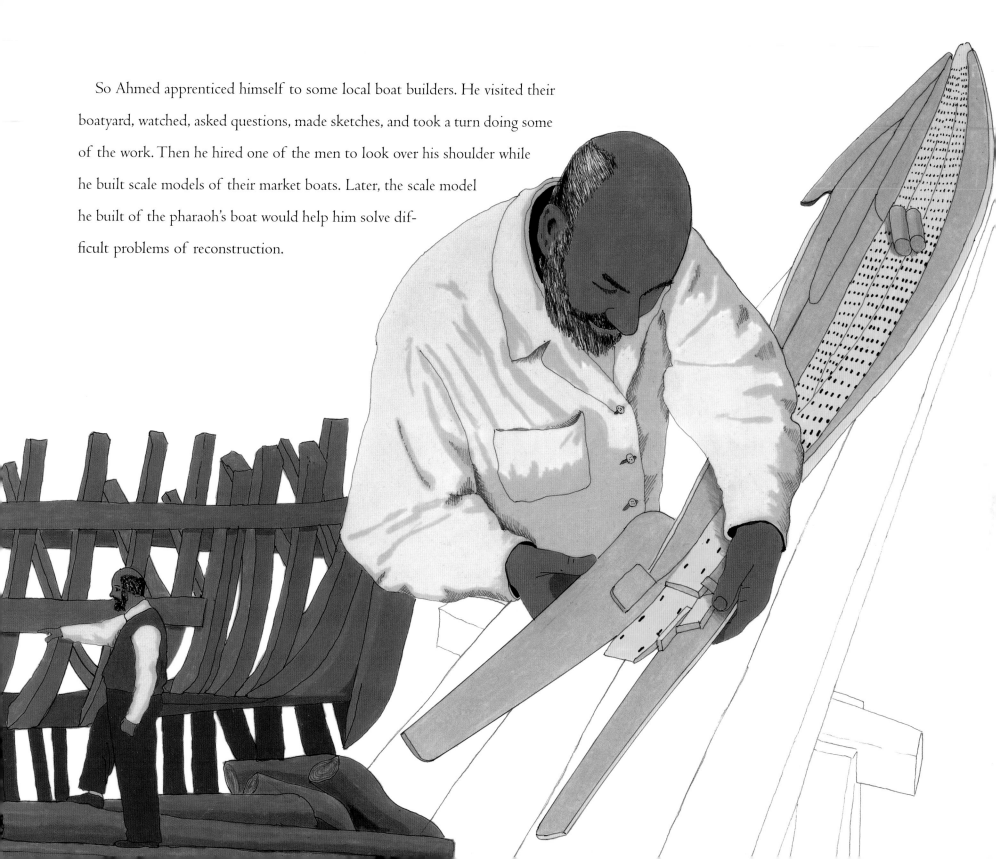

Removing the 651 largest pieces of the boat from the pit was like a giant game of pick-up sticks. Some of the timbers had become dry and brittle; many were cracked and broken; a few had turned to dust. Ahmed devised a simple scaffold that would enable him and his workmen to be raised and lowered into the pit and work above the boat so as not to step on the old wood. Before moving a timber, the workmen had to be sure it would not jar, twist, bend, or upend fragile pieces near it. If they thought that might happen, adjacent pieces were braced and cushioned. Removing the longest planks—almost seventy feet— required special care; they could snap of their own weight.

Before the boat could be pieced back together, entirely new restoration techniques had to be invented, tested, and analyzed. Measuring, drawing, photographing, and restoring the many parts took more than a decade before the first assembly could even be attempted. This careful recording eventually led to solving many baffling mysteries of how the ship went back together. For instance, they discovered the meaning of the four markings, one of which appeared on each of the largest pieces.

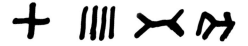

Comparing the symbols with the location of each piece in the pit, Ahmed's team realized that the four symbols represented the four quarters of a boat—fore and aft, starboard and port. Each piece belonged to a specific quarter.

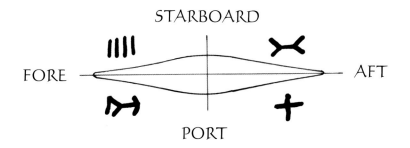

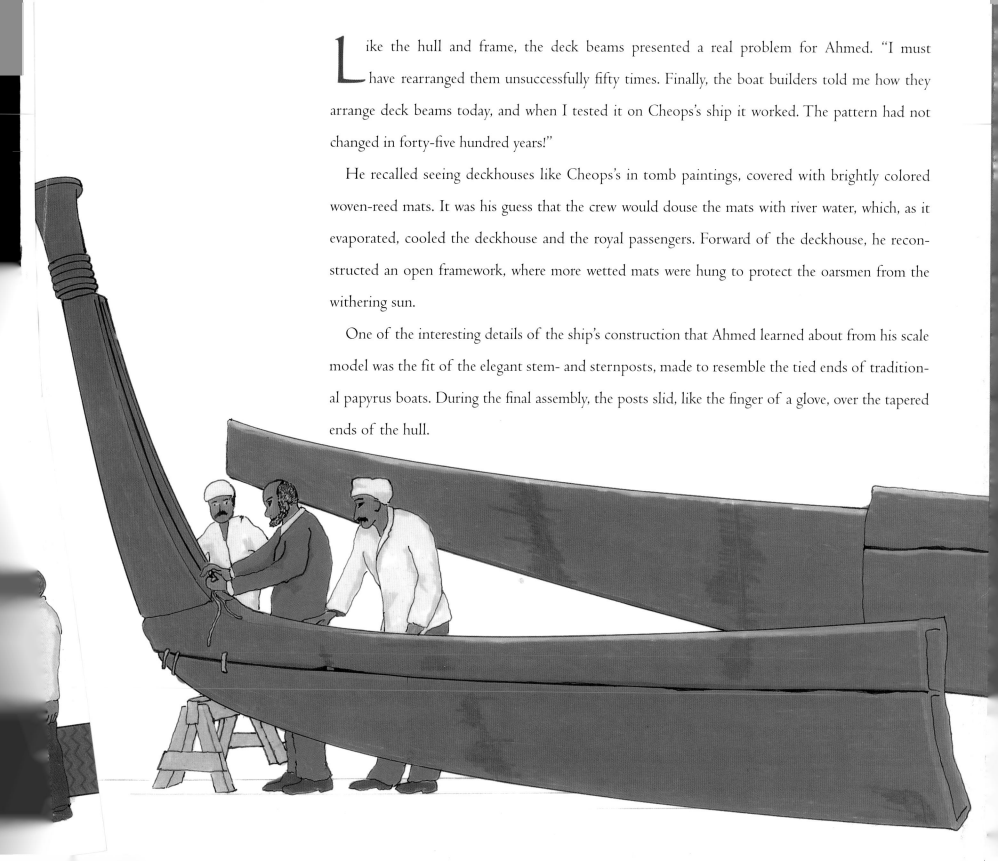

Like the hull and frame, the deck beams presented a real problem for Ahmed. "I must have rearranged them unsuccessfully fifty times. Finally, the boat builders told me how they arrange deck beams today, and when I tested it on Cheops's ship it worked. The pattern had not changed in forty-five hundred years!"

He recalled seeing deckhouses like Cheops's in tomb paintings, covered with brightly colored woven-reed mats. It was his guess that the crew would douse the mats with river water, which, as it evaporated, cooled the deckhouse and the royal passengers. Forward of the deckhouse, he reconstructed an open framework, where more wetted mats were hung to protect the oarsmen from the withering sun.

One of the interesting details of the ship's construction that Ahmed learned about from his scale model was the fit of the elegant stem- and sternposts, made to resemble the tied ends of traditional papyrus boats. During the final assembly, the posts slid, like the finger of a glove, over the tapered ends of the hull.

Other periods have their high points, but none compete with [Cheops's time] for beauty and for knowing when to stop. The workmanship and finish were of the finest level, and yet the crafts-men achieved a simplicity of detail and line that is an inspiration.

—Hag Ahmed Youssef Moustafa

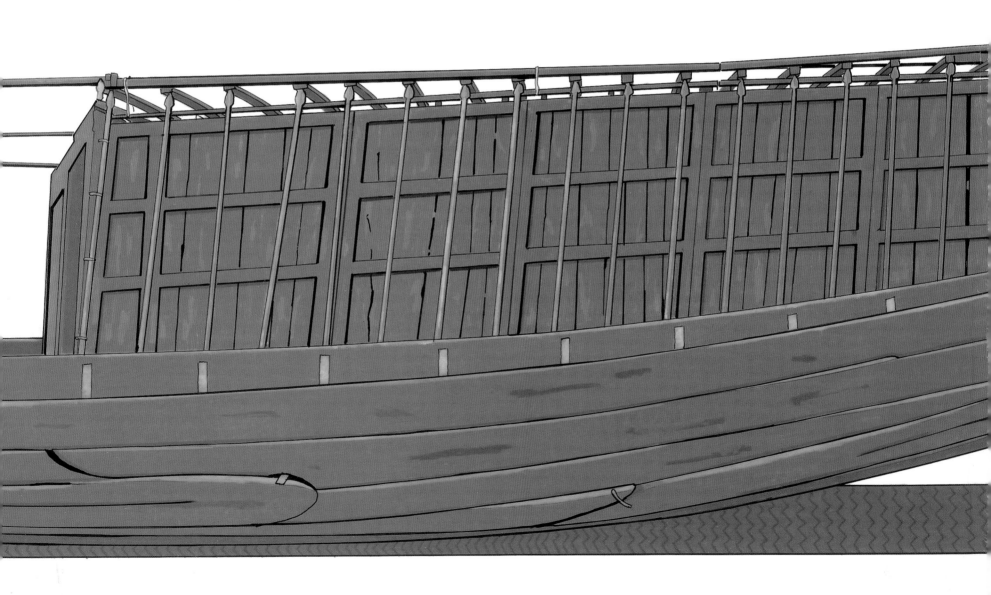

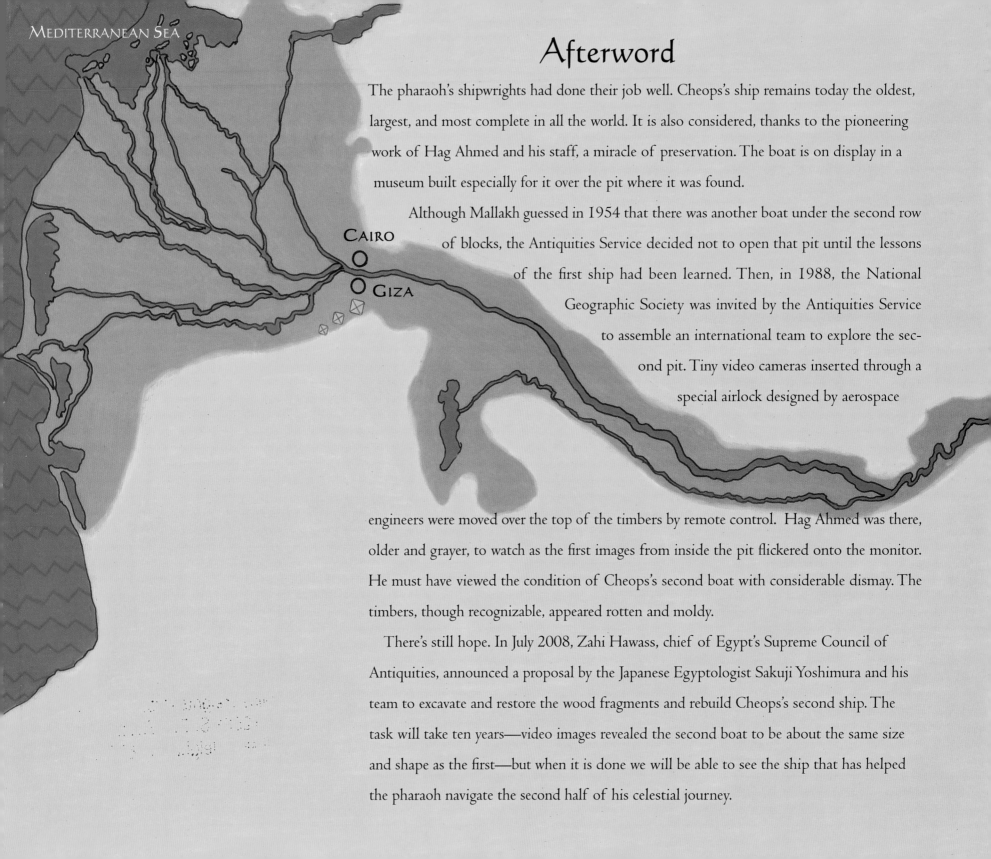

CAIRO

GIZA

Afterword

The pharaoh's shipwrights had done their job well. Cheops's ship remains today the oldest, largest, and most complete in all the world. It is also considered, thanks to the pioneering work of Hag Ahmed and his staff, a miracle of preservation. The boat is on display in a museum built especially for it over the pit where it was found.

Although Mallakh guessed in 1954 that there was another boat under the second row of blocks, the Antiquities Service decided not to open that pit until the lessons of the first ship had been learned. Then, in 1988, the National Geographic Society was invited by the Antiquities Service to assemble an international team to explore the second pit. Tiny video cameras inserted through a special airlock designed by aerospace engineers were moved over the top of the timbers by remote control. Hag Ahmed was there, older and grayer, to watch as the first images from inside the pit flickered onto the monitor. He must have viewed the condition of Cheops's second boat with considerable dismay. The timbers, though recognizable, appeared rotten and moldy.

There's still hope. In July 2008, Zahi Hawass, chief of Egypt's Supreme Council of Antiquities, announced a proposal by the Japanese Egyptologist Sakuji Yoshimura and his team to excavate and restore the wood fragments and rebuild Cheops's second ship. The task will take ten years—video images revealed the second boat to be about the same size and shape as the first—but when it is done we will be able to see the ship that has helped the pharaoh navigate the second half of his celestial journey.

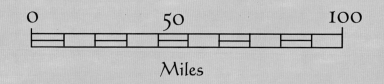

0   50   100

Miles

N

○ THEBES

ASWAN
○

Acknowledgments

I never got to meet Hag Ahmed; he died several years before I visited the boat and began to write his story. But thanks to Paul and Marcelle Lipke, I feel I know him well. They spent a year with Hag Ahmed in Cairo, recording his memories of the restoration and reconstruction and studying thousands of documents, drawings, and photographs, some of which they copied and generously shared with me. Their suggestions and insights, along with Paul's marvelous detailed study *The Royal Ship of Cheops* and Peter Schmid's precise technical illustrations, made this book possible as well as immensely enjoyable.

Other sources of details for my story and drawings were Nancy Jenkins's *The Boat Beneath the Pyramid: King Cheops' Royal Ship,* and the photographs by John Ross; Cheryl Ward's "Sacred and Secular: Ancient Egyptian Ships and Boats"; Björn Landström's *Skeppet* and *Ships of the Pharaohs* and photographs from the collections of the Egyptian Antiquities Service. I found the answer to the mystery of the second boat in *National Geographic* (April 1988).

My thanks also to Loren Fisher for sharing with me his knowledge of things Egyptian and for his translations of the tomb inscriptions accompanying the drawings. To editor Kelly Loughman, whose enthusiasm for my story brightens every page. And, finally, to Hussein Nour El-din, for taking me to see the boat, explaining so well the life of the ancient Egyptians, sharing his own Muslim heritage, and warmly welcoming me to Cairo and Giza.

Copyright © 2009 by David Weitzman

Houghton Mifflin Books for Children is an imprint of Houghton Mifflin Harcourt Publishing Company.

www.hmhbooks.com

The text of this book is set in Centaur MT. The illustrations are colored pencil and pen and ink on matte film.

Library of Congress Cataloging-in-Publication Control Number 2008036081
ISBN 978-0-547-05341-7

Printed in China
SCP 10 9 8 7 6 5 4 3 2